VEGA

MW00881742

PRESSURE

COOKER

COOKBOOK

Quick, Easy and Delicious 100% Plant Based Recipes on Foodi Pressure Cooker (Zero Animal Products, with Images)

Clarion Wilson

Copyright ©2019 By Clarion Wilson

Disclaimer

The content and information contained in this book has been compiled from sources deemed reliable, and it is accurate to the best of the Author's knowledge, information and belief. However, the Author cannot guarantee its accuracy and validity and cannot be held liable for any errors and/or omissions. Further, changes are periodically made to this book as and when needed. Where appropriate and/or necessary, you must consult a professional (including but not limited to your doctor, attorney, financial advisor or such other professional advisor) before using any of the suggested remedies, techniques, or information in this book.

Table of Contents

Introduction

Veganism, as a global phenomenon, became a popular choice for millions of people around the globe. What's driving more and more conscious people to choose a plant-based lifestyle? Health, ethical, altruistic, environmental reasons? In case you were wondering why people worldwide follow a vegan diet, the medical database contains a large amount of information.

Convenience is always sought for when it comes to cooking. Today no one can spend most of his time and efforts in the kitchen due to many restraints. Hence it is best to equip our lives with smart technology and tricks. The Ninja Foodi meets all the demands you require in a modern cooking device. The Ninja Foodi has the feature of an Instant Pot, Air fryer and Slow cooker all in one pot, this is convenient and saves you space in your kitchen.

I have been Vegan for over 7 years now and have been creating Vegan recipes. When I purchased my Ninja Foodi from the store few months ago, I started trying out my vegan recipes on them and they were cool. So, I made a compilation and also contacted my Vegan community for ideas to come up with the recipes in this book

Most of the times, I laugh glancing at most vegan cookbooks and recipes I see online. I see most of them listing cheese, butter, honey, heavy oil, meats and dairy products on their ingredients. All these are non-vegans' products.

Most of the times, I laugh glancing at most vegan cookbooks and recipes I see online. I see most of them listing cheese, butter, honey, heavy oil, meats and dairy products on their ingredients. All these are non-vegans' products.

This book serves as a beginner's guide to the Vegan Diet and Ninja Foodi. It contains over 200 100% Vegan recipes with no traits of animal product. Recipes have nutritional information and images for visualization.

Chapter One: Introduction Ninja Foodi

The traditional pressure cookers evolved impressively with time due to advance technology and tech innovation. Ninja Foodi has raised the bar in the pressure cooker category and has been ranked as one of the most favorite kitchen gadgets of today. The Ninja food is a contemporary pressure cooker integrated with various exclusive features like multi-pressure levels, digital display, timer and a keep warm feature. The most prominent feature that makes Ninja Foodi an extraordinary gadget is that it doubles as an air fryer that not just pressure cooks the food fast but also makes it super crispy. In other words, Ninja Foodi has been developed with Tender Crisp Technology, and can act as multi-use cooker. Mainly, it's a nice blend of air fryer and pressure cooker; however, an inclusion of other important features makes it function beyond that.

How Ninja Foodi Work

Pressure Release Valve
Easily release pressure.

Pressure Lid
Quickly tenderize and cook ingredients.

Reversible Rack
Use to steam, or reverse to broil.

Cook & Crisp™ Basket
4-quart nonstick, ceramic-coated basket fits 3 lbs of French fries.

Crisping Lid
Use to finish off pressure cooked recipes or to air fry your food.

Cooking Pot
6.5-quart nonstick, ceramic-coated cooking pot fits a 6-lb roast.

14 Levels of Safety
Passed rigorous testing to earn UL safety certification, giving you peace of mind.

The Ninja Foodi is one of the most attractive pressure cookers on the market nowadays. As an electric multi-cooker, it can perform various advanced cooking tasks such as pressure cooking, slow cooking, sautéing, searing, steaming, air frying, broiling, baking, warming, and even dehydrating. This easy-to-use device is designed to cook your food faster and healthier than traditional methods. Essentially, the Ninja Foodi is a sealed pot that creates pressure by heating liquid such as water or stock. In this way, it maintains the steam and constant internal pressure inside the pot. On the other hand, it comes with a cooking basket that allows you to fry your food with less oil. When it comes to the interior, the Ninja

Foodi has a ceramic-coated non-stick cooking pot and Cook & Crisp™ basket. It also comes with five stovetop temperature settings, dual pressure levels (high and low) and a user-friendly control panel that is easy to read. It enables you to set perfect cooking time, temperature and pressure level according to your personal preferences and favorite recipes.

Rules for Using the Ninja Foodi

1. Read a manual before using the product.
2. The Ninja Foodi is equipped with multiple safety features (even 14 levels of safety), but you should always be careful with pressure cookers.
3. Do not touch hot surfaces; always use handles and kitchen gloves.
4. Keep your hands and face away from the steam coming from the vent.
5. Be careful when removing the pressure lid; never force it open.
6. Do not fill the cooking pot beyond the recommended level at 2/3 full (or 1/3 full if you cook rice, grains, legumes, and dried beans).
7. As for pressure cooking, simply put your ingredients into the inner pot. Seal the PRESSURE LID and choose the desired function. Afterwards, release pressure from your cooker.
8. As for air frying, add your ingredients to the cooking basket, use the crisping lid and choose the desired function, time and temperature. Press the START/STOP button.

Function Buttons in Foodi Crisping Pressure

PRESSURE COOK – this is the most common function of your Ninja Foodi. How does it work? Here are basic steps:

1. Lock the pressure lid and turn the valve to seal;

2. Set the time and adjust temperature;

3. Wait for unit to build pressure;

4. When cooking is complete, the unit will beep so you can release the pressure; otherwise, unit will switch to the KEEP WARM function. This is the common function because you can control the time and temperature yourself and customize them according to your recipe or your personal preferences.

STEAM – this is an ideal program for delicate foods such as vegetables and seafood because they require short cooking time, preheated steam, and precise temperature control. You will be able to prepare fresh or frozen foods in less than no time. For instance, beets can be completely steamed in about 15 minutes, cabbage in 3 minutes, and cauliflower will be cooked in 2 minutes. Use a reversible rack that comes with your device in lower position.

SLOW COOK – you can have your dinner ready for when you come back home. Use this program for slow cooking and simmering.

SAUTE/SEAR – go one step further and use this mode to brown meats, sauté vegetables, and thicken the sauces and gravies; cooking on this setting can maximize flavors, too.

AIR CRISP – you can "fry" your favorite food without drenching them in oil. How does it work? Use Cook & Crisp™ basket with this function. You can adjust the temperature between 300 degrees F to 400 degrees F according to your needs. Further, you can open the lid during cooking process to shake the cooking basket or toss ingredients with silicone tipped-tongs for even cooking; when done, put the cooking basket back into the pot and secure the crisping lid. Cooking will automatically resume after that. If you tend to fry smaller chunks that could fall through the rack, you can wrap them in a piece of foil. Use this function to reheat your meals, too.

BAKE/ROAST – this program works as a typical oven; you can make casseroles, frittatas, and desserts. You can choose a temperature between 250 degrees F and 400 degrees F.

BROIL – this program uses intense direct heat to cook food. It provides a caramelizing and charring that give your food that distinct flavor. You do not have to heat your grill or oven to achieve great results in the kitchen – just use a reversible rack in higher position.

DEHYDRATE – you can dehydrate your food in an easy way and have your own dried fruits and vegetables all year long. You can choose the temperature between 105 degrees F and 195 degrees F. Use the Cook & Crisp™ basket and a dehydrating rack.

START/STOP – Use this button to Start or Cancel a function or turn off your Multi-cooker. When you pressure-cooking time is up, it will automatically switch to Keep Warm.

KEEP WARM – once cooking is complete; the unit will automatically switch to this mode and start counting. It will take 12 hours. To keep your food safe, pay attention to food safety temperatures. To prevent your meal from drying out, just leave the lid closed.

TEMP ARROWS: Use the up and down TEMP arrows to adjust the cook temperature and/or pressure level.

TIME ARROWS: Use the up and down TIME arrows to adjust the cook time.

QUICK PRESSURE RELEASE – turn the pressure release valve to the VENT position to release pressure quickly.

NATURAL PRESSURE RELEASE – steam will release from the unit as it cools down. A natural pressure release can take up to 20 minutes, depending on the amount of food. When the pressure is fully released, the red float valve will drop down, so you can remove the lid.

STANDBY MODE: After 10 minutes with no interaction with the control panel, the unit will enter standby mode.

What You Can Do with Ninja Foodi

What can you cook with your Ninja Foodi? The simple answer is – you can cook almost everything in your Ninja Foodi thanks to its tender-crisp technology and multiple functions. Based on the foregoing, we can conclude that there are just so many possibilities.

RICE & GRAINS are extremely versatile. Give your family a new way of enjoying grains! Extremely picky eaters will love rice and grains that are cooked in the cooking pot and then finished off in the cooking basket using the AIR CRISP function. The flavors are infused into rice and grains while cooking in the Ninja Foodi. Before pressure cooking, rinse your grains in a fine mesh strainer under running tap water. After releasing pressure, stir and fluff rice for about 1 minute. You can use PRESSURE button to cook rice and grains fast, while maintaining tenderness. You can cook white rice in 2 to 3 minutes; wild rice will take 22 minutes, while brown rice will take 15 minutes. Further, you can cook polenta in 4 minutes and steel-cut oats in 11 minutes.

BEANS should be soaked 8–12 hours before pressure cooking. Of course, you can cook dried beans without soaking in your Ninja Foodi. It will take about 30 minutes and beans will triple in quantity when cooked. Therefore, for 1 cup of dried beans, you will have 3 cups of cooked beans.

MEATS & POULTRY can be cooked to perfection in your Ninja Foodi. Tough cuts of meat such as chuck roast, flank steak or brisket turn out succulent, juicy and delicious. This will remind you of your grandma's kitchen. Rest the meat for about 5 minutes before slicing in order to seal in the natural juices.

VEGETABLES maintain their authentic flavor. The Ninja Foodi is an amazing one-pot kitchen appliance that uses the latest flavor infusion technology to cook delicious and nutritious vegetable dishes. This advanced technology uses superheated steam to lock in all the aroma and nutrients in your food. It is almost magic!

FROZEN FOODS. You can put them directly into the cooking pot without defrosting them; just add an extra 10 minutes to the cook time.

How to Use the Foodi Crisping Pressure Cooker

1. Preparing your ingredients

Prepare ingredients according to the directions in the pressure-cooking recipe you have selected. For extra flavor, use the brown or sauté functions first, just like you would when cooking with conventional cookware. For instance, brown the meat and vegetables for a stew, before adding other liquids and cooking under pressure. Be sure to deglaze the pot, scraping up any browned bits clinging to the bottom with a small amount of wine, broth or even water, so they loosened, adding flavor to your food, as well as discouraging scorching.

2. Add Liquid

After the aromatics softened, add the remaining ingredients and pour liquid, into the cooker body, as specified in the recipe or timetable. This fluid is usually water. However, some recipes will call for other liquids, such as wine.

3. Lock the lid

Assemble the pressure lid by aligning the arrow on the front of the lid with the arrow on the front of the cooker base. Then turn the lid clockwise until it locks into place. Make sure the pressure release valve on the lid is in the SEAL position.

4. Select the function

Select the function, according to the recipe. Press the START/STOP button to begin. Your Foodi will begin to build pressure, indicated by the rotating lights. The unit will begin counting down when it is fully pressurized

5. Turn off the cooker and release the pressure.

When the countdown is finished, the Foodi will beep, automatically switch to the Keep Warm mode, and begin counting up. After the pressure-cooking time has finished, turn off the cooker by selecting "Start/Stop" button. You can release the pressure two ways: quick release and natural release, according to the recipe or timetable instructions.

6. Air Frying and Finish the dish

In some cases, after releasing pressure and carefully removing the lid, some dishes need Air fry, bake, roast, or broil to evenly crisp and caramelize meals to golden-brown perfection, finish with a crisp to create Crisp meals or simmer to help thicken, reduce, or concentrate the liquid; others require to add more ingredients to finish the recipe.

Cleaning & Maintenance of Your Foodi Pressure cooker

Cleaning: Dishwasher & Hand-Washing

The unit should be cleaned thoroughly after every use.

1. Unplug the unit from the wall outlet before cleaning.
2. **NEVER** put the cooker base in the dishwasher or immerse it in water or any other liquid.
3. To clean the cooker base and the control panel, wipe them clean with a damp cloth.
4. The cooking pot, silicone ring, reversible rack, Cook & Crisp Basket, and detachable diffuser can be washed in the dishwasher.
5. The pressure lid, including the pressure release valve and anti-clog cap, can be washed with water and dish soap. **DO NOT** wash the pressure lid or any of its components in the dishwasher, and **DO NOT** take apart the pressure release valve or red float valve assembly.
6. To clean the crisping lid, wipe it down with a wet cloth or paper towel after the heat shield cools.
7. If food residue is stuck on the cooking pot, reversible rack, or Cook & Crisp Basket, fill the pot with water and allow to soak before cleaning. **DO NOT** use scouring pads. If scrubbing is necessary, use a non-abrasive cleanser or liquid dish soap with a nylon pad or brush.
8. Air-dry all parts after each use.

Removing & Reinstalling the Silicone Ring

To remove the silicone ring, pull it outward, section by section, from the silicone ring rack. The ring can be installed with either side facing up. To reinstall, press it down into the rack section by section. After use, remove any food debris from the silicone ring and anti-clog cap.

Keep the silicone ring clean to avoid odor.

Washing it in warm, soapy water or in the dishwasher can remove odor. However, it is normal for it to absorb the smell of certain acidic foods. It is recommended to have more than one silicone ring on hand.

NEVER pull out the silicone ring with excessive force, as that may deform it and the rack and affect the pressure-sealing function. A silicone ring with cracks, cuts, or other damage should be replaced immediately.

Useful Tips for Your Foodi Crisping Pressure cooker

1. For consistent browning, make sure ingredients are arranged in an even layer on the bottom of the cooking pot with no overlapping. If ingredients are overlapping, make sure to shake half way through the set cook time.

2. **Watch out about overfilling.** Your Ninja foodi should not be completely filled. Ever! You need space for pressure and/or steam to build up. Whether you are filling it with food or fluid, always make sure there is plenty of space from the top.

3. For smaller ingredients that could fall through the reversible rack, we recommend first wrapping them in a parchment paper or foil pouch.

4. **DO NOT** use a damaged removable cooking pot, silicone ring or lid Replace before using.

5. When switching from pressure cooking to using the crisping lid it is recommended to empty the pot of any remaining liquid for best crisping results.

6. Press and hold down the Time Up or Down arrows to move faster through the display to get to your desired time.

7. **Unplug from outlet when not in use and before cleaning**. Allow to cool before putting on or taking off parts.

8. Use the Keep Warm mode to keep food at a warm, food-safe temperature after cooking. To prevent food from drying out, we recommend keeping the lid closed and using this function just before serving. To reheat food, use the Air Crisp function.

9. **DO NOT** touch hot surfaces. Appliance surfaces are hot during and after operation. To prevent burns or personal injury, ALWAYS use protective hot pads or insulated oven mitts and use available handles and knobs

10. To have your unit build pressure quicker, set it to SEAR/SAUTÉ HIGH. Once ready to pressure cook, press the PRESSURE button and continue as you normally would.

11. **NEVER** use **SLOW COOK** setting without food and liquids in the removable cooking pot.

12. **DO NOT** attempt to open the lid during or after pressure cooking until all internal pressure has been released through the pressure release valve and the unit has cooled slightly. If the lid will not turn to unlock, this indicates the appliance is still under pressure - DO NOT force lid open. Any pressure remaining can be hazardous. Let unit naturally release pressure or turn the Pressure Release Valve to the VENT position to release steam. Take care to avoid contact with the releasing steam to avoid burns or injury. When the steam is completely released, the red float valve will be in the lower position allowing the lid to be removed.

13. **Do not leave the house when it is on**. Unlike with a traditional slow cooker, the Ninja Foodi reaches high temperatures, can carry a high voltage, and involves literal pressure

Ninja Foodi Cook Settings

FUNCTION	Time	Temp
Air Crisp	1-60 minutes	300 to 400
Bake/Roast	1min to 4hr	250 to 400
Broil	1-30 minutes	Auto Set at 450. Not adjustable
Dehydrate	1hr to 12hr	105 to 195
Pressure	1min to 4hr	Lo
		Hi
Steam	10 20 30 min	No temp option
Slow Cook	6hr to 12hr	Lo
		Hi
Sear/Sauté	No time option	Lo
		LOMD
		MD
		MD Hi
		Hi

Foodi Air Crisp Conversion Chart

Type	Food	Crisping Temp	Crisping Lid Time, Fresh	Crisping Lid Time, Frozen	Oil?	Notes
VEGGIES						
	Frozen Hash Browns	350		20 min	Lightly Sprayed	
	Frozen Tater Tots	400		12 min		
	French Fries	400	20 min	400 @15- 20 min	Spray	Soak 30 min prior if fresh cut
	Corn on the Cob	360	25 min			Foil Wrapped/Turn 1X
	Roasted Cauliflower	350	15 min		Rub with Oil	Add 1 cup water to bottom
	Green Beans	350	12 min			
	Tomatoes	370	10-12 min			
	Peppers	400	12 min			
	Roasted Asparagus	370	10 min			Preheat 2 min
	Whole Potato	370	35 min			
	Potato, 1/2 length	360	30 min			
	Red Potatoes	350	25 min			Shake a few times
	Potato Wedges	390	16 min		Spray	
	Baked Apples, Cored	360	20 min			Cut in half
BAKING						
	Air Fried Corn Chips	370	5 min		Lightly Sprayed	
	Canned Biscuits	330	6 min			Baking dish
	Frozen Biscuits	350		12 min		Baking dish
	Cake	300	25 min/Foil 10 more			Baking dish
	Quiche	360	20-22 min			Baking dish
	Muffins	390	15-18 min			Baking dish
	Sweet snacks	320	20 min			Baking dish

Foodi Pressure Cooker Chart

Type	Food	Crisping Temp	Crisping Lid Time, Fresh	Crisping Lid Time, Frozen	Oil?	Notes
VEGGIES						
	Frozen Hash Browns	350		20 min	Lightly Sprayed	
	Frozen Tater Tots	400		12 min		
	French Fries	400	20 min	400 @15-20 min	Spray	Soak 30 min prior if fresh cut
	Corn on the Cob	360	25 min			Foil Wrapped/Turn 1X
	Roasted Cauliflower	350	15 min		Rub with Oil	Add 1 cup water to bottom
	Green Beans	350	12 min			
	Tomatoes	370	10-12 min			
	Peppers	400	12 min			
	Roasted Asparagus	370	10 min			Preheat 2 min
	Whole Potato	370	35 min			
	Potato, 1/2 length	360	30 min			
	Red Potatoes	350	25 min			Shake a few times
	Potato Wedges	390	16 min		Spray	
	Baked Apples, Cored	360	20 min			Cut in half
BAKING						
	Air Fried Corn Chips	370	5 min		Lightly Sprayed	
	Canned Biscuits	330	6 min			Baking dish
	Frozen Biscuits	350		12 min		Baking dish
	Cake	300	25 min/Foil 10 more			Baking dish
	Quiche	360	20-22 min			Baking dish
	Muffins	390	15-18 min			Baking dish
	Sweet snacks	320	20 min			Baking dish

Wild Rice	20		High	Natural	20-30	1 cup water per 1 cup rice
White Rice	12					1 cup water per 1 cup rice
Veggies						
Asparagus	1		High	Normal	3	
Bell Pepper	4		High	Normal	3	
Black Eyed Peas	7		High	Natural	20-30	
Black Beans	26		High	Natural	20-30	Cover with water
Broccoli	5		High	Normal	3	
Cauliflower Florets	3		High	Normal	3	
Corn on Cob	4		High	Natural	3	
Green Beans	3		High	Normal	3	
Mushrooms	5		High	Normal	3	
Potatoes, baby small	6		High	Normal	3	
Potatoes, Sweet	10		High	Natural	20-30	1 cup water + rack
Potatoes, whole	13		High	Normal	3	1 cup water + rack
Pinto Beans	26		High	Natural	20-30	Cover with water
Veggie Chunks	3		High	Normal	3	1 cup water + rack

Chapter Two: Introduction to Vegan Diet

Veganism

Veganism sounds intimidating. It shouldn't. It isn't half as bad as it's made out to be. First of all, it's nothing like you think it is. It is not a cult. It is not a group of ascetics that are trying to deprive themselves of all pleasure. Nor it is a bunch of new-age flagellants punishing themselves for the world's sins. Yes, some see it as a religion, but there are extremists in every group. At its core, veganism is nothing more than a lifestyle choice. It focuses on making us live respectfully and in harmony with the world and ourselves. Nothing more, nothing less. And yes, in decades past being vegan was hard. It took a great deal of self-discipline as you were depriving yourself of a lot of textures and flavors. These days, as the recipes in this book demonstrate, it is a lot easier. Science and culinary experimentation have created many products that can replace animal products. There are numerous vegan products available in most western countries. Thankfully, companies have also taken to labeling in vegan-friendly manners. That certainly helps! What's more, you don't have to go vegan all at once. Veganism isn't an on off switch. It's more of a journey. It is fine to come to it gradually, one meal at a time. If you want, start with trying to stick to it once or twice a week and scale up from there. Every so often you'll back slide. That's alright. As long as the road continues onward and upward, you have nothing to be ashamed of. After all, by embarking on this adventure you're already doing more than most.

The Vegan Diet

The idea of the vegan diet is straightforward. First off, it aims to reduce the pressure on your digestive system by choosing proteins and nutrient sources that are easy to digest. Second, it aims to promote a way of exercising that is more in line with how we used to move before this modern age. These two things together will give our bodies a large health boost. Note that we're not aiming at a particular form of exercising. You can do whatever you like, just as long as you vary it. Don't look to bulk yourself up and don't work only on muscle definition.

As for the diet, it isn't about you depriving yourself of calories or eating the same thing three times a week without fail. Instead it is about wholeness. Digestion, health, mind and mood are interlinked and all together determine your wellbeing.

Veganism is both a diet and a lifestyle choice. It's about avoiding the consumption of animal and animal products in any way, shape or form.

For these reasons, the vegan diet is devoid of all animal products, including meat, eggs and dairy.

Vegan diets tend to be higher in dietary fiber, magnesium, folic acid, vitamin C, vitamin E, iron, and phytochemicals; and lower in dietary energy, saturated fat, cholesterol, long-chain omega-3 fatty acids, vitamin D, calcium, zinc, and vitamin B12.

Foods You Can Eat on Vegan Diet

- Soy milk, almond milk, coconut milk, cashew milk, oat milk
- Fruits
- Vegetables
- Legumes, such as lentils, peas and beans
- Nuts and seeds
- Olive oil and olives

Foods Not Allowed on Vegan Diet

- Seafoods
- All meats and poultry products
- Cheese
- Milk
- Yoghurt
- Butter
- Fish
- Cream
- Eggs
- Sweets made with and dairy products
- Foods that includes lard and fish oil

Foods to Limit

1. **Vegan sweeteners:** Vegan or not, molasses, date syrup, agave syrup and maple syrup are still regarded as added sugars. Consuming them in excess may increase your risk of developing medical issues such as heart disease and obesity

2. **Vegan protein bars:** Most vegan protein bars contain high amounts of refined sugar. What's more, they usually contain an isolated form of protein, which lacks the nutrients you'd find in the plant it was extracted from.

3. **Mock meats and cheeses:** Processed foods generally contain lots of additives. They also provide you with far fewer vitamins and minerals than whole, protein-rich plant foods like beans, lentils, peas, nuts and seeds.

4. **Vegan junk food:** Vegan ice cream, candy, cookies, chips and sauces generally contain just as much added sugar and fat as their non-vegan counterparts. Plus, they contain almost no vitamins, minerals and beneficial plant compounds.

5. **Some dairy-free milks:** Sweetened dairy-free milks generally contain a good amount of added sugar. opt for the unsweetened versions instead.

Do's of a Vegan Diet

1. **Fill Up on Veggies:** They are full of fiber and micronutrients that are critical to keeping you satiated and full of energy. Even if you're the kind of person who will eat meat forever until the day you die, eat more veggies (especially leafy green ones)

2. **Include Probiotics:** Dairy products contain probiotics which are good bacteria that live in our gut. When eliminating dairy products out of your diet, it's important that you find other vegan-friendly probiotic sources: coconut yogurt (with active cultures) and fermented foods like sauerkraut and kombucha.

3. **Track Your Food: When** transitioning to a new eating style, or anytime for that matter, it's important to track your food so you know you're getting the macro- and micronutrients your body needs to fuel your life.

Don'ts of Vegan Diet

Don't Become A Carb-O-Vore: You need protein in your diet, so it's critical that you're not just eating vegan pasta all the time. You need to be creative to make sure you're also including enough protein and fats in your diet. Try our vegan recipes like Berry Banana Smoothie Bowl and Pumpkin Sweet Potato Soup so you'll never get bored if you choose to go the vegan route.

Don't Become Vegan to Be Like Your Friend or Favorite Celebrity: Your diet should be something that makes you feel good, gives you energy and doesn't make you feel like you're craving everything in sight. It's okay to try out new eating habits, but be honest with yourself and decide honestly if it's the right choice for you.

Don't Think That Something Is Healthy Just Because It's Vegan: There are so many vegans processed and packaged foods out there that can sabotage your goals. You still need to be a label-reader and make sure there aren't any sneaky sugars, extra sodium or preservatives that won't serve your goals.

Benefits of a Vegan Lifestyle

Can you follow a vegan diet and still get all necessary nutrients? Are there the evidence-based benefits of a vegan diet? If you are not a vegan, it is perfectly normal to have doubts about dietary change. In the following lines, I will try to explain the findings from the scientifically credible studies that have proven the benefits of a vegan dietary regime.

1. **Health benefits of a vegan diet**. Following a balanced plant-based diet ensures many health benefits, including the prevention of many chronic diseases. A vegan menu is loaded with whole foods such as fresh fruits,

nutrient-dense vegetables, legumes, whole grains, and nuts. The nutrients in those foods are vital for the maintenance of a healthy body. In fact, people who eat mostly plants as part of their daily diet have a reduced risk of many serious diseases.

However, you should consume a range of different foods to make sure you get essential vitamins, minerals, and amino acids. In other words, you should provide your body with essential nutrients that must come from food; the human body cannot synthesize essential nutrients on its own or it cannot make them in sufficient quantity. As for the carcinogenicity of the consumption of red meat and processed meat, The World Health Organization (WHO) announced, "Meat consists of multiple components, such as harm iron.

Meat can also contain chemicals that form during meat processing or cooking. For instance, carcinogenic chemicals that form during meat processing include N-nitrous compounds and polycyclic aromatic hydrocarbons. Cooking of red meat or processed meat also produces heterocyclic aromatic amines as well as other chemicals including polycyclic aromatic hydrocarbons, which are also found in other foods and in air pollution. Some of these chemicals are known or suspected carcinogens, but despite this knowledge it is not yet fully understood how cancer risk is increased by red meat or processed meat."

A plant-based diet can help you prevent many serious diseases. If you consume hyper-processed food, sugar, trans fats, white flour, chemicals, and inflammatory foods, meat, and dairy products, you're more likely to develop chronic diseases. On the other hand, cooking at home can help you adopt healthy eating habits and lose weight in a natural way. A plant-based diet is loaded with fiber, whole grains, and fresh fruits that boost your metabolism and improve digestion, as well as make you feel fuller longer. Further, fresh fruits and vegetables are lower in calories, fats and bad cholesterol than animal products.

Numerous studies have shown that eating a vegan diet may help prevent prostate cancer colon cancer, and breast cancer. It can also cure fatigue, arthritis, osteoporosis, reflux, cardiovascular disease, chronic allergies, eczema, psoriasis, macular degeneration, and autoimmune disease. A vegan diet high in fruits and vegetables can help you regulate blood pressure (it can cut systolic blood pressure by more than 10 points). Obviously, our food is the best medicine.

2. **A well-planned vegan diet can make you stronger and more energetic.**

Besides being super healthy, eating plant-based diet also provides many physical benefits. What's more, a plant-based diet leads to lower Body Mass Index (BMI). A vegan diet may help you lose weight in a natural way. The Adventist Health Study (AHS) has proven that vegans have lower BMI than people who eat animal products such as dairy, eggs, seafood, and especially red meat.

If you tend to gain lean muscle, you should focus on eating foods that can help you build tissues and exercising regularly. Numerous plant-based foods can help you build muscle and get stronger. Vegan muscle-building foods include soybeans, black, kidney and pinto beans, quinoa, brown rice, chickpeas, buckwheat, peanuts, almonds, tofu, protein powders (hemp, soy, and pea). Focus on nutritious, protein-packed foods that can stimulate muscle growth.

Put simply, if your goal is to be happy, healthy and strong, use energy from a plant-based food.

3. **A well-Balanced Vegan Diet can make you Look and Feel Fantastic**

"You are what you eat", it may sound like a cliché, but it is true! Your diet can significantly affect the health of your skin. Luckily, there are easy solutions to make your skin glow from the inside out. The best way to keep your skin healthy is by ensuring that you're eating a variety of good and nutritious foods. Vitamin C is needed for a healthy, radiant skin. A vegan diet is loaded with foods with high vitamin C content such as citrus fruits, bell peppers, leafy greens, broccoli, strawberries, and kiwi fruit. Walnuts are a great source of omega-3 and omega-6 fatty acids, which make them a great food for healthy skin. Further, nuts and seeds are an excellent source of vitamin E, which is an important antioxidant and anti-aging vitamin. Vitamin A is also a powerful vitamin for younger looking skin. You should eat carrots, apricots, mango, and broccoli. Forget the Botox and eat your way to a healthier and younger skin. Top anti-aging foods include mushrooms, avocado, blueberries, pomegranate, watermelon, tomato, figs, red cabbage, cucumber, sweet potatoes. As for beverages, green tea, red wine, and almond milk can protect your skin from aging. When it comes to the herbs and spices, you should eat parsley, garlic, turmeric, and saffron. These foods are not only great for your skin, but they also help you stay young and healthy. Ultimately, when you look great, you feel great!

Chapter Three: Vegan Ninja Foodi Recipes

Vegetable Soup

Serves: 10

Preparation Time: 35 minutes

Ingredients

- 2 tsp sea salt
- 1/2 tsp black pepper
- 1 tsp basil dried leaves
- 1 tsp thyme dried leaves
- 1 tsp garlic powder
- 1 tsp onion powder
- 1 lb. carrots sliced
- 1 cup 15 bean mix dry
- 4 cups water
- 1/2 Tbsp minors vegetable base
- 1 cup onion diced
- 14.5 ounces fire roasted tomatoes
- 2 tsp sea salt
- 2 celery
- 12 ounces corn frozen
- 12 ounces peas frozen
- 12 ounces green beans frozen

Directions

1. Peel and slice carrots into 1/4" slices. Dice onion and celery to 1/2-1" dice. Rinse the beans

2. Combine all ingredients into the inner pot of the Ninja Foodi and stir.

3. Put on the pressure lid and make sure the valve is to seal. Pressure cook on high for 30 minutes.

4. When the 30 minutes is up, allow to natural release for 3-6 minutes and then manually release the remaining pressure.

5. Serve and Enjoy!

Nutritional Information: Calories 175, Carbs 35g, Fiber 5g, Protein 9g

Fresh Beet Greens

Serves: 4

Preparation: 13 minutes

Ingredients

- 2 bunches beet greens fresh
- 1/2 cup water
- 1/4 teaspoon black pepper fresh ground
- 1 garlic clove minced
- 1/2 teaspoon kosher salt

Directions

1. Trim the beet leaves from the beets. Cut the leaves and stems into about 2-inch pieces.
2. Wash the greens thoroughly. They can be very gritty and sandy.
3. Pour 1/2 cup water into the Ninja Foodi liner pot.
4. Place the greens in the pot and season with 1/2 teaspoon of kosher salt, 1/4 teaspoon fresh ground black pepper, and 1 minced garlic clove. Stir to distribute the seasonings.
5. Place the pressure-cooking lid in place and lock. Set to high pressure and cook for 3 minutes.
6. Quick release by carefully turning the pressure release control to vent.
7. Serve and enjoy!

Nutritional Information: Calories 2, Carbs 1g, Fats 1g, Protein 1g

Crispy Tofu

Serves: 4

Preparation Time: 60 minutes

Ingredients

- 1 tsp. seasoned rice vinegar
- 2 tbsp. low sodium soy sauce
- 2 tsp. toasted sesame oil
- 1 block firm tofu, sliced into cubes
- 1 tbsp. potato starch
- Cooking spray

Directions

1. In a bowl, mix the vinegar, soy sauce, and sesame oil.
2. Marinate the tofu for 30 minutes. Coat the tofu with potato starch.
3. Spray the Ninja Foodi basket with oil. Seal the crisping lid.
4. Choose the air crisp setting. Cook at 370 degrees for 20 minutes, flipping halfway through.
5. You can serve with soy sauce and vinegar dipping sauce. Enjoy!

Nutritional Information: Calories 137, Carbs 24g, Fats 3.4g, Protein 2.3g

Crispy Cauliflower Bites

Serves: 4

Preparation Time: 12 minutes

Ingredients

- 3 garlic cloves, minced
- 1 tbsp. olive oil
- 1/2 tsp. salt
- 1/2 tsp. smoked paprika
- 4 cups cauliflower florets

Directions

1. Place in the ceramic pot the Foodi Cook and Crisp basket.
2. Place all ingredients in a bowl and toss to combine.
3. Place the seasoned cauliflower florets in the basket.
4. Close the crisping lid and press the Air Crisp button before pressing the START button.
5. Adjust the cooking time to 10 minutes.
6. Give the basket a shake while cooking for even cooking.
7. Serve and enjoy!

Nutritional Information: Calories 130, Carbs 7g, Fats 12.4g, Protein 4.3g

Curried lentil stuffed Peppers

Preparation Time: 40 mins

Serve: 4

Ingredients

- 4 Large Green Bell Peppers
- 1 Yellow Onion, diced
- 8 oz. Baby Bella or Cremini Mushrooms, diced
- 1 cup dry Lentil
- 1 cup dry Brown Rice
- 3 cups Vegetable Broth
- 1 ½ tbsp. Salt-Free Curry Powder
- 1 tsp Garlic Powder
- 2 tbsp. Fresh Ginger, minced
- 3/4 cup Raw Cashews, roughly chopped
- 3 tbsp. Tamari

Instructions

1. First, wash and prep your vegetables. Core the Bell Pepper and finely dice the tops. Add all of the ingredients to the pot of the Ninja Foodi, except for the Tamari, Cashews, and cored Peppers; stir well.

2. Close the Pressure lid on the Foodi, and set the pressure release valve to SEAL. Select PRESSURE and set to HIGH, then cook for 15 minutes; press START/STOP to begin.

3. When pressure cooking is complete, naturally release the pressure for 10 minutes, then quick release the remaining pressure by moving the valve to the VENT position. Carefully remove the lid once all of the pressure has released; add the Tamari and Cashews to the pot and stir well, but save some Cashews to top the Peppers with.

4. Equally stuff the mixture into the 4 cored Bell Peppers, and top with the remaining Cashews. Quickly rinse the pot out, place the Peppers in the Cook and Crisp Basket, and then place the basket in the pot.

5. Close the crisping lid of the Foodi and select BAKE/ROAST. Set the temperature to 360°F, and set the time to 15 minutes. Select START/STOP to begin.

6. Once cooking is complete, serve immediately. Store leftovers in the fridge for up to 7 days.

Everyday Use Veggie-Stock

Preparation Time: 100 minutes

Serves: 1 quart

Ingredients

- 1 onion, quartered

- 2 large carrots, peeled and cut into 1-inch pieces

- 1 tablespoon olive oil

- 12 ounces mushrooms, sliced

- ¼ teaspoon salt

- 3 and ½ cups water

Directions

1. Take cook and crisp basket out of the inner pot, close crisping lid and let it pre-heat for 3 minutes at 400 degrees F on Bake/Roast settings

2. While the pot heats up, add onion, carrot chunks in the Cook and Crisp basket and drizzle vegetable oil, toss well

3. Place basket back into the inner pot, close crisping lid and cook for 15 minutes at 400 degrees F on Bake/Roast mode

4. Make sure to shake the basket halfway through

5. Remove basket from pot and add onions, carrots, mushrooms, water and season with salt

6. Lock pressure lid and seal the valves, cook on HIGH pressure for 60 minutes

7. Release the pressure naturally over 10 minutes

8. Line a colander with cheesecloth and place it over a large bowl, pour vegetables and stock into the colander

9. Strain the stock and discard veggies

10. Enjoy and use as needed!

Nutritional Information: Calories 45, Carbs 3g, Fats 4g, Protein 0g

Balsamic Broccoli

Preparation Time: 15 minutes

Serves: 4

Ingredients

- 1 broccoli head, florets separated

- 1 tablespoon olive oil

- 6 garlic cloves, minced

- 1 tablespoon balsamic vinegar

- Salt and black pepper to the taste

Directions

1.   In your Foodi's basket, mix all the broccoli with the rest of the ingredients, toss, and cook on Air Crisp mode at 390 degrees F for 10 minutes.

2.   Divide between plates and serve.

Nutritional Information: Calories 173, Carbs 9g, Fats 4g, Protein 6g

Brussels Sprouts

Serves: 4

Preparation Time: 5 minutes

Ingredients

- 1 lb. Brussels sprouts
- 1/4 cup pine nuts
- Salt and pepper to taste
- Olive oil
- 1 cup water

Directions

1. Pour the water into the Foodi. Set the steamer basket. Put the Brussels sprouts into the steamer basket.

2. Close and lock the lid. Press the Pressure button. Set the pressure to HIGH and set the time to 3 minutes.

3. When the timer beeps, turn the valve to Venting to quick release the pressure

4. Transfer the Brussels sprouts into a serving plate, season with olive oil, salt, pepper, and sprinkle with the pine nuts

Nutritional Information: Calories 137, Carbs 24g, Fats 3.4g, Protein 2.3g

Roasted Vegetables with Tamarind Dip

Preparation Time: 10 minutes

Serves: 6

Ingredients

- 1/4 cup balsamic vinegar
- 1 tsp black pepper
- Salt to taste
- 1 cup potatoes, cubed
- 1 cup green bell pepper, cubed
- 1 cup carrots, sliced
- 1 cup onion, quartered
- 1 cup cauliflower florets
- 1 cup broccoli florets 3
- /4 cup peas

For Dip

- 1/2 cup tamarind paste
- 1 clove garlic, minced
- 1/2 tsp black pepper

For Garnishing

- 1/4 cup sesame seeds

Directions

1. Mix all the dip ingredients to a bowl; set aside.
2. In a large mixing bowl, combine all the vegetables.
3. In another small mixing bowl, mix balsamic vinegar, black pepper and salt; mix until well combined.
4. Add the dressing into the vegetables, toss until they are well coated.
5. Preheat the foodi to air crisp mode, for 5 minutes.

6. Place the vegetables into the basket and bake/roast at 400F for 10 minutes.

7. When finished cooking, transfer the veggies to a serving dish.

8. Top with sesame seeds and serve with dip.

Nutritional Information: Calories 49, Carbs 10.52g, Fats 0.18g, Protein 1.59g

Homemade Carrot & Turmeric Soup

Preparation time: 55 mins

Servings: 2

Ingredients

- 1 tbsp. olive oil
- 1 medium-sized onion, chopped
- 2 garlic cloves
- 1/4 tsp turmeric powder
- 500g carrots, peeled and chopped
- 1.2l vegetable stock
- Handful fresh coriander
- Salt & pepper, to taste

Instructions

1. Set your Ninja Foodi to Sauté mode on MEDIUM settings add 1 tbsp. olive oil, add the chopped onion, crushed garlic, then Sauté until softened.
2. Stir in the turmeric powder and the chopped carrots – add the vegetable stock along with salt and pepper to taste, bring it to a boil then reduce the temperature.
3. Cover and Slow cook for approximately 30 minutes until the carrots are tender.
4. Put to one side and allow to cool to room temperature.
5. Pour the ingredients into the jug of your Ninja Kitchen blender, add fresh coriander and blitz until smooth – adjust seasoning if needed.
6. Pour back into a pan and heat through until warm.

Coconut, Peanut Butter & Chocolate Bites

Preparation Time: 20 mins

Servings: 8

Ingredients

- For the Peanut Butter Base
- 100g oats
- 1 tsp cinnamon
- 3 tbsp. peanut butter
- 4 tbsp. maple syrup
- 2 tbsp. coconut oil, melted

For the Coconut Filling

- 3 tbsp. coconut oil
- 3 tbsp. maple syrup
- 70g desiccated coconut

For the Chocolate Topping

- 3 tbsp. coconut oil
- 3 tbsp. maple syrup
- 5 tbsp. cacao powder
- Cacao nibs and coconut chips to decorate

Instructions

1. Place all of the ingredients for the base into your Ninja Kitchen Nutri Ninja blender and pulse quite a few times until the mixture comes together in a slightly sticky flapjack mixture.

2. Press into the base of a lined 15cm x 20cm tin or tub with your hands evenly. Set aside.

3. Next, melt the coconut oil and whisk in the maple syrup and coconut to form a slightly thick but spreadable mixture. Spoon this over the base to cover and use the back of a spoon to spread and pat down. Chill while you make the topping.

4. Melt the coconut oil then whisk in the maple syrup and cacao powder to form a smooth chocolate sauce. Pour this over the coconut layer to cover. Sprinkle over the cacao nibs and coconut then place in the fridge for at least 2 hours to set.

Remove from the tub or tin and onto a chopping board. Cut into 8-10 pieces and enjoy!

Green Lasagna Soup

Preparation Time: 30 minutes

Serves: 4

Ingredients

- ½ pound broccoli; chopped
- 3 lasagna noodles
- 1 carrot; chopped
- 2 garlic cloves minced
- 1 cup tomato paste
- 1 cup tomatoes; chopped
- ¼ cup dried green lentils
- 2 cups vegetable broth
- 1 cup leeks; chopped
- 1 teaspoon olive oil
- 2 teaspoon Italian seasoning
- salt to taste

Directions

1. Warm oil on Sear/Sauté. Add garlic and leeks and cook for 2 minutes until soft; add tomato paste, carrot, Italian seasoning, broccoli, tomatoes, lentils, and salt. Stir in vegetable broth and lasagna pieces.
2. Seal the pressure lid, choose Pressure, set to High, and set the timer to 3 minutes. Press Start.
3. Release pressure naturally for 10 minutes, then release the remaining pressure quickly. Divide soup into serving bowls and serve.

Nutritional Information: Calories 253.5, Carbs 22.8g, Fats 6.5g, Protein 24g

Steamed Broccoli and Carrots with Lemon

Preparation Time: 10 minutes

Serves: 3

Ingredients

- 1 cup broccoli florets
- 1/2 cup carrots, julienned
- 2 tbsp. lemon juice
- Salt and pepper, to taste

Directions

1. Place the Ninja Foodi Cook and Crisp reversible rack inside the ceramic pot.
2. Pour water into the pot. Toss everything in a mixing bowl and combine. Place the vegetables on the reversible rack.
3. Close the pressure lid and set the vent to SEAL.
4. Press the Steam button and adjust the cooking time to 10 minutes. Do a quick pressure release. Serve and enjoy!

Nutritional Information: Calories 35, Carbs 8.1g, Fats 0.3g, Protein 1.7g

Stewed Cabbage

Preparation Time: 40 minutes

Serves: 7

Ingredients

- 13 ounces cabbage
- 2 red bell pepper
- ¼ Chile pepper
- 1 cup tomato juice
- 1 tablespoon olive oil
- 1 teaspoon salt
- 1 teaspoon paprika
- 1 teaspoon basil
- ½ cup dill, chopped

Directions

1. Wash the cabbage and chop it into tiny pieces. Sprinkle the chopped cabbage with the salt, paprika, and basil and mix well using your hands.
2. Transfer the chopped cabbage in the pressure cooker. Add tomato juice, olive oil, and chopped dill. Chop the Chile pepper and red bell pepper.
3. Add the vegetables to the pressure cooker and mix well. Close the pressure cooker lid and cook the dish on" Pressure" mode for 30 minutes. When the dish is cooked, let it rest briefly and serve.

Nutritional Information: Calories 46, Carbs 6.6g, Fats 2.2g, Protein 1g

Chili with Cornbread Crumble

Preparation: 1 hour

Serves: 8

Ingredients

- 4 large carrots, chopped
- 5 stalks celery, chopped
- 3 medium russet potatoes, chopped
- 1½ cups cooked (1 15-ounce can rinse and drained) kidney beans
- 1½ cup cooked (1 15-ounce can rinse and drained) black beans
- 1 cup corn kernels
- 1 tablespoon tamari
- 1 tablespoon olive oil
- 1 medium onion, diced
- 3 cloves garlic, minced
- salt and black pepper to taste
- Cayenne powder (Optional), added to taste for spicy chili
- 1 batch Vegan Cornbread Mini Muffin batter
- 1 (28-ounce) can crushed tomatoes
- 1 cup vegetable broth
- 1-3 tbs chili powder, added to taste

Toppings

- fresh cilantro
- vegan sour cream

Directions

1. Preheat the oven to 375°. Grease a mini muffin tray.

2. Prepare the flax "egg' by stirring ground flaxseed in a small bowl together with warm water. Allow it sit 10 minutes before using.

3. In a large bowl, whisk together the cornmeal, flour, baking powder and salt.

4. Stir together the coconut oil, nondairy milk, maple syrup, and apple cider vinegar in a small bowl.

5. Add the contents of the small bowl to the large and mix thoroughly. Fold in the corn kernels.

6. Spoon the batter into the mini muffin wells, until they are just full. Bake until the tops are crisp and you're able to stick a wooden toothpick in and it comes out clean, about 15 minutes.

Root Vegetable Soup & Roasted Chickpeas

Preparation Time: 50 mins

Servings: 4

Ingredients

- 1 tbsp. oil

- 1 onion

- 2 cloves of garlic

- 2 sticks of celery, chopped

- 2 tsp mixed herbs

- 1 tsp turmeric

- 3 carrots, sliced or chopped

- 2 sweet potatoes, peeled and chopped

- 600ml vegetable stock

- Salt & black pepper

- For the Roasted Chickpeas

- 1 x can chickpeas, drained well

- 1 tbsp. oil

- 2 tsp paprika

- Pinch of chili powder (optional)

- Salt & black pepper

Instructions

1. Select SEAR/SAUTE and set to HIGH on your Ninja Foodi. After 5 minutes add the oil, onion, garlic and celery and cook for 5 minutes, stirring occasionally.

2. Add the herbs, turmeric, carrots and sweet potatoes and continue cooking for another 5 minutes.

3. Pour in the stock and salt and pepper then place the pressure lid on top making sure it is in the SEAL position.

4. Select PRESSURE and set to HIGH and set timer for 20 minutes.

5. Meanwhile, mix everything together in a bowl for the chickpeas and bake in a preheated Foodi at 190 degrees C for 15 minutes to roast nicely.

Ninja Foodi Cabbage

Preparation: 22 minutes

Serves: 4

Ingredients

- 3/4 tsp Old Bay
- 1 tsp garlic salt
- olive oil spray
- 1 head cabbage cut into 4ths
- 1 c water

Directions

1. Rinse cabbage, cut off stem, and take outer leaves off. Discard.
2. Cut head into 4 equal parts and put into your Ninja Foodi air fryer basket.
3. Add cup of water to your inner pot, put basket inside pot. Set to high pressure for 1 minute, then do a quick release.
4. Remove lid and drain water.
5. Put basket with cabbage inside back into pot. Spray with olive oil spray and sprinkle with seasonings. Close air fryer lid.
6. Set to 400 degrees for 16 minutes (or until the outer leaves are as crispy as you'd like them).
7. Enjoy!

Nutritional Information: Calories 58, Carbs 13g, Fats 1g, Protein 3g

Vegan Chili

Preparation Time: 45 mins

Servings: 2

Ingredients

- 1/2 cup

- 2 medium potatoes

- olive oil

- garlic

- salt

- black pepper

- cayenne pepper

Instructions

1. 1/2 cup water in the pot, pierced two medium potatoes and cooked for 10 minutes at high pressure; used a quick release.

2. Brushed the potatoes with olive oil, garlic, salt, black pepper, and cayenne pepper; air crisped at 350°F for 10 minutes.

3. Bumped the temp up to 400°F and cooked for 15 minutes longer.

Buffalo Cauliflower Steak

Preparation Time: 45 mins

Servings: 2

Ingredients

- 1 head of cauliflower
- 1 cup of water
- 1 teaspoon olive oil
- 1 teaspoon lime chicken salt
- 2 cloves garlic, minced
- 2 teaspoons Franks Red-hot seasoning powder

Instructions

1. Put 1 head of cauliflower and 1/4-ish cup of water in your Foodi and cook on low pressure for 3 minutes, quick release.

2. While the cauliflower was under pressure, prepare 1/2 cup sauce in a measure cup (1 teaspoon olive oil, 1 teaspoon lime chicken salt, 2 cloves garlic, minced, 2 teaspoons Franks Red-hot seasoning powder, water).

3. After pressure is released, pour the buffalo sauce over the cauliflower. Air Crisp for 15 minutes at 390°F.

Breakfast Porridge with Barley and Strawberries

Preparation Time: 25 minutes

Serves: 8

Ingredients

- 2 cups pot barley, rinsed and drained
- 3 teaspoons vegetable oil
- 1/2 teaspoon kosher salt
- 6 cups water
- 2 cups fresh strawberries
- 1 cup cashews, chopped
- Juice of 1/2 fresh lime

Directions

1. Combine the barley, oil, salt, and water in the inner cooking pot.
2. Secure the pressure lid; press the PRESSURE button and cook for 15 minutes at High Pressure.
3. Once cooking is complete, use a natural release; remove the lid carefully.
4. Drain the barley and return it to the pot.
5. Add the remaining ingredients and stir to combine.
6. Secure the crisping lid and choose the AIR CRISP function.
7. Set the temperature to 380 degrees F and set the time to 9 minutes; press the START/STOP button.
8. To serve, divide prepared barley salad among individual bowls. Enjoy!

Nutritional Information: Calories 301, Carbs 14.4g, Fats 47.2g, Protein 7.8g

Winter Rice Salad

Serves: 6

Preparation Time: 35 minutes

Serves: 6

Ingredients

- 2 cups wild rice, rinsed and drained
- 1-pound Acorn squash, cubed
- 1 tablespoon minced Chile pepper
- 1/2 cup carrots, chopped
- 1/2 cup parsnip, chopped
- 1 turnip, chopped
- 3 teaspoons olive oil
- 1 ½ teaspoons salt
- 6 cups water

For the Dressing

- 1/4 cup extra-virgin olive oil
- Freshly squeezed juice of 1/2 lemon
- Sea salt and freshly ground black pepper, to taste
- 1/2 teaspoon cayenne pepper

Directions

1. Add rice, salt and oil to the inner cooking pot. Pour in 4 cups of water. Secure the pressure lid; press the PRESSURE button and cook for 17 minutes at High Pressure.
2. Once cooking is complete, use a natural release; remove the lid carefully.
3. Place a reversible rack over rice. Place the squash, carrots, parsnip, Chile pepper and turnip on the rack.

4. Secure the crisping lid and choose the AIR CRISP function. Set the temperature to 390 degrees F and set the time to 14 minutes; press the START/STOP button.

5. Drizzle the dressing over your salad.

6. Serve well-chilled.

Nutritional Information: Calories 214, Carbs 29g, Fats 4g, Protein 10.3g

Tofu Rancheros with Veggies and Little Face Salsa

Preparations Time: 55 mins

Servings: 4

Ingredients

For the Spice Crusted Tofu:

- 1 - 20 0z container High Protein Tofu or Super Firm Tofu (or firm that's been pressed for at least 1 hour), cut into cubes
- 1 teaspoon ground cumin powder
- 1 teaspoon ground chili powder or less if you prefer mild foods
- 1/2 teaspoon smoked paprika
- 1/4 teaspoon salt or to taste

For the Salsa Beans:

- 1 15.5 ounce can organic black beans, drained (save liquid to make brownies or chocolate cookies)
- 1/4 cup Little Face Big Taste Jalapeno Cilantro Salsa or your fav mild salsa
- 1/8 to 1/4 teaspoon liquid smoke to suit your taste (or use 1/8 teaspoon smoked paprika)
- 1/8 teaspoon jalapeno powder (or chipotle or cayenne) powder
- 1/8 teaspoon cumin powder
- salt to taste

For the Veggie Topping:

- 1/3 cup grated carrot
- 1/3 cup grated zucchini

- 1/3 cup grated yellow squash
- 1/8 teaspoon salt
- pinch black pepper

For the Base:

- 4 large flour or gluten-free tortillas I used Ezekiel brand
- 1 cup shredded vegan cheese or make oil free with my cauliflower queso

Directions

Make the Spice Crusted Tofu:

1. Toss the tofu cubes with the cumin, chili powder, smoked paprika, and salt.
2. Preheat your Foodi to 390° in the Air Crisp functions. Once it's hot, add the coated tofu to your air crisp basket.
3. Set the cooking time to 5 minutes and when the time is up, shake or stir the tofu. Repeat for an additional 5 minutes.

Make the Salsa Beans:

- Mix all the ingredients together in a small bowl.

Prepare the Base:

1. Take 2 tortillas and put on a baking sheet while preheating the Bake/Roast to 350 degrees. Sprinkle (or spread) 1/4 cup vegan cheese on top of each tortilla. Put 1/4 of the salsa beans in the middle of the tortilla and bake for 15 minutes.
2. This will warm the beans and make the tortilla crunchy.

3. Once warm add on the Spiced Crusted Tofu, the shredded veggie topping, chopped tomatoes or other veggies you'd like to pile on like avocado or shredded lettuce.

4. Top it all off with a heaping spoonful of Little Face Salsa!

Vegan fried ravioli in the Foodi

Preparation Time: 22 mins

Servings: 4

Ingredients

- 1/2 cup panko bread crumbs
- 2 teaspoons nutritional yeast flakes
- 1 teaspoon dried basil
- 1 teaspoon dried oregano
- 1 teaspoon garlic powder
- Pinch salt & pepper
- 1/4 cup aquafaba liquid from can of chickpeas or other beans*
- 8 ounces frozen or thawed vegan ravioli
- Spritz cooking spray
- 1/2 cup marinara for dipping

Instructions

1. On a plate, combine panko bread crumbs, nutritional yeast flakes, dried basil, dried oregano, garlic powder, salt, and pepper.
2. Put aquafaba into a small separate bowl.
3. Dip ravioli into aquafaba, shake off excess liquid, and then dredge in bread crumb mixture. Make sure that the ravioli gets fully covered.
4. Move the ravioli into the air Crisp basket. Continue until all of the ravioli has been breaded. Be careful not to overlap the ravioli too much in the air crisp, so that they can brown evenly. (If necessary, air fry in batches.)
5. Spritz the ravioli with cooking spray.

6. Set Foodi to 390 degrees. Air Crisp for 6 minutes. Carefully flip each ravioli over. (Don't just shake the basket. If you do, you'll lose a lot of bread crumbs.) Cook for 2 more minutes.

7. Remove ravioli and serve with warm marinara for dipping.

Quinoa and Potato Salad

Serves: 6

Preparation Time: 25 minutes

Ingredients

- 1/4 cup white balsamic vinegar

- 1 tbsp. Dijon mustard

- 1 tsp. sweet paprika

- 1/2 tsp. ground black pepper

- 1/4 tsp. celery seeds

- 1/4 tsp. salt

- 1/4 cup olive oil

- 1 1/2 pounds tiny white potatoes, halved

- 1 cup blond (white) quinoa

- 1 medium shallot, minced

- 2 medium celery stalks, thinly sliced

- 1 large dill pickle, diced

Directions

1. Whisk the vinegar, mustard, paprika, pepper, celery seeds and salt in a large serving bowl until smooth.

2. Whisk in the olive oil in a thin, steady stream until the dressing is fairly creamy.

3. Place the potatoes and quinoa in the Ninja Foodi Multicooker; add enough cold tap water so that the ingredients are submerged by 3 inches (some of the quinoa may float).

4. Lock the lid on the Ninja Foodi Multicooker and then cook for 10 minutes. To get 10-minutes cook time, press "Pressure" button and use the Time Adjustment button to adjust the cook time to 10 minutes.

5. Use the quick-release method to bring the pot's pressure back to normal.

6. Unlock and open the pot. Close the crisping lid. Select BROIL, and set the time to 5 minutes. Select START/STOP to begin.

7. Cook until top has browned. Drain the contents of the pot into a colander lined with paper towels or into a fine-mesh sieve in the sink. Do not rinse.

8. Transfer the potatoes and quinoa to the large bowl with the dressing. Add the shallot, celery, and pickle; toss gently and set aside for a minute or two to warm up the vegetables. Serve and enjoy!

Oil-Free Chips (Garlic Parm Flavor)

Prep Time: 45mins

Ingredients

- 2 Large Red Potatoes
- 2 tsp salt
- 4 garlic cloves crushed or minced
- 2 tbsp. homemade vegan parmesan

Instructions

1. Thinly slice the potatoes. I recommend using a mandolin (I use a 1.5mm blade.)
2. Place the sliced potatoes in a bowl and fill with water. Mix in 2 teaspoons of salt. Let soak for 30 minutes.
3. Drain and rinse the potatoes. Pat dry.
4. Toss the potatoes with crushed garlic and vegan parmesan.
5. Layer half of the potato slices in the basket
6. In no more than 4 or so layers. Don't overload the basket or the chips won't cook evenly.
7. Fry at 170 degrees F for 20-25 minutes, or until dry to the touch and no longer flimsy. Stir and toss the basket every 5 minutes or so.
8. Bump the temperature up to 400 degrees Fahrenheit and fry for an additional 5 minutes or until the potatoes have become crunchy.
9. Remove from the Foodi and top with more vegan parm or salt.
10. Repeat for the other half of the potato slices.
11. Snack away!

Potato Wedges

Preparation Time: 40 minutes

Serves: 4

Ingredients

- 1 lb. potatoes, sliced into wedges
- 1 tsp. olive oil
- Salt and pepper, to taste
- 1/2 tsp. garlic powder

Directions

1. Coat the potatoes with oil. Season with salt, pepper and garlic powder
2. Add the potatoes in the Ninja Foodi basket. Cover with the crisping lid. Set it to air crisp.
3. Cook at 400 degrees F for 16 minutes, flipping halfway through.
4. You can serve with vegan cheese sauce. Enjoy!

Nutritional Information: Calories 179, Carbs 36.2g, Fats 2.6g, Protein 2.8g

Oil-Free Chips (Garlic Parm Flavor)

Prep Time: 45 minutes

Ingredients

- 2 Large Red Potatoes
- 2 tsp salt
- 4 garlic cloves crushed or minced
- 2 tbsp. homemade vegan parmesan

Instructions

1. Thinly slice the potatoes. I recommend using a mandolin (I use a 1.5mm blade.)
2. Place the sliced potatoes in a bowl and fill with water. Mix in 2 teaspoons of salt. Let soak for 30 minutes.
3. Drain and rinse the potatoes. Pat dry.
4. Toss the potatoes with crushed garlic and vegan parmesan.
5. Layer half of the potato slices in the basket
6. In no more than 4 or so layers. Don't overload the basket or the chips won't cook evenly.
7. Fry at 170 degrees F for 20-25 minutes, or until dry to the touch and no longer flimsy. Stir and toss the basket every 5 minutes or so.
8. Bump the temperature up to 400 degrees Fahrenheit and fry for an additional 5 minutes or until the potatoes have become crunchy.
9. Remove from the Foodi and top with more vegan parm or salt.
10. Repeat for the other half of the potato slices.
11. Snack away!

Crispy Tofu Nuggets

Preparation Time: 35 mins

Servings: 4

Ingredients

- 1 x 400g block firm tofu

- 1/3 cup oat milk

- 3 tbsp. almond flour

- 2 tbsp. plain white gluten-free flour

- 1 tbsp. nutritional yeast

- 1 tsp vegetable stock powder

- 1/4 tsp paprika

- 1/8 tsp garlic granules

- 1/8 tsp turmeric powder

Instructions

1. Drain the tofu and press in a tofu press to remove more water for crispier tofu. Use a tofu press. Alternatively, wrap the tofu in a clean kitchen towel and place it between two chopping boards, then pile several heavy books on top and leave it for 2-3 hours.

2. Once the tofu has been drained/ pressed, use your hands to break it into 'nugget' sized chunks. You can cut it into pieces if you would prefer, but I think the ragged edges are better to hold the coating and make them look like typical chicken nuggets.

3. Pour the oat milk into a shallow bowl.

4. In a separate shallow bowl, mix together all of the remaining ingredients.

5. Take a piece of tofu and coat it in milk, followed by the coating. Make sure that all of the sides are covered. Then place it in the Ninja Foodi Cook & Crisp Basket. Repeat until all of the tofu is coated.

6. Seal the lid of the Foodi. Select 'Air Crisp' at 400F for 20 minutes. Then press Start.

7. Once the nuggets are ready you can serve them with chips and beans or a side salad.

Baked Bananas

Serves: 4

Preparation Time: 12 minutes

Ingredients

- 4 firm bananas, peeled and halved

- 1/4 cup maple syrup

- 1 tbsp. ground cinnamon

- 1-piece fresh ginger, grated

- 1 1/2 tsp. nutmeg

Directions

1. Place in the ceramic pot the Foodi Cook and Crisp reversible rack.

2. In a bowl, season the bananas with maple syrup, ground cinnamon, ginger, and nutmeg.   Place the bananas on the rack.

3. Close the crisping lid and press the Bake/Roast button before pressing the START button.

4. Adjust the cooking time to 10 minutes.

5. Serve and enjoy!

Nutritional Information: Calories 183, Carbs 42.2g, Fats 0.9g, Protein 1.4g

Peanut Butter and Jam Brownies

Prep: 20 mins/Cook: 40 mins

Servings: 9

Ingredients

- 250g oats (use gluten free if required)
- 70g cacao powder
- 1 tsp baking powder
- 1/4 tsp salt
- 75ml maple syrup
- 90ml non-dairy milk (I use unsweetened oat milk)
- 60ml apple sauce
- 50ml coconut oil (melted)
- 1 tsp vanilla extract
- 50g dairy free dark chocolate chunks
- 100g smooth peanut butter plus 1 tbsp. coconut oil (combined and melted in microwave for 45 seconds)
- Strawberry jam (use store bought or homemade chia seed jam seed recipe as follows)
- 200g strawberries (cut into small chunks)
- 1 tbsp. chia seeds
- 3 tbsp. maple syrup

Instructions

1. Preheat Foodi to 350°F and grease a square tin (or an 8-inch baking pan). with some coconut oil.
2. In your food processor, blitz your oats into a fine flour.
3. Next add cocoa powder, baking powder, salt and blitz again.

4. Pour in maple syrup, non-dairy milk, apple sauce, coconut oil and vanilla extract. Blitz again until combined.

5. Gently fold the chocolate chunks into the mixture.

6. Empty mixture into tin, before covering completely with the melted peanut butter.

7. If you are making your own jam, combine the strawberries and maple syrup in a saucepan on a medium heat. Let simmer for 5 minutes before, mashing into a jam like consistency and stirring in chia seeds. Let simmer for a further 5 minutes.

8. Add dollops of jam onto the peanut butter and using a knife draw swirls to create a marble effect.

9. Place into Foodi for 40 minutes, before taking out and leaving to cool for 30 minutes.

10. Cut into squares and enjoy

Sweet Potato Wedges & Smoked Paprika Hummus

Preparation time: 50 mins

Servings: 4

Ingredients

- 2-3 large sweet potatoes, cut into wedges
- 2 tbsp. oil
- 2 tsp paprika
- 2 tsp mixed herbs
- Black pepper & salt

For the Hummus

- 1 x can chickpeas, drained and rinsed
- 1 clove of garlic
- Juice of 2 lemons
- 2 spring onions
- 2 tsp smoked paprika
- 2 tsp cumin
- 2 tbsp. oil

Instructions

1. Mix together the sweet potato wedges with the other ingredients in a bowl to coat well.
2. Place the potatoes into the Cook & Crisp basket. Close the lid on your Ninja Foodi and select AIR CRISP to 200 degrees C and set time to 30 minutes. Check after 15 minutes to see how they are getting on.
3. Meanwhile, place the hummus ingredients into your Ninja Kitchen chopper and pulse until you have a smooth dip. Chill until needed.
4. Once the potatoes are soft and crisp on the outside, serve with the hummus to dip into and enjoy!

Sweet Sriracha Carrots

Serves: 4

Preparation Time: 27 minutes

Ingredients

- 2 tablespoons sriracha
- 1 cup water
- 1 teaspoon sugar
- 2 tablespoons olive oil
- ½ cup dill
- 1-pound carrots
- 1 teaspoon oregano

Directions

1. Wash the carrots, peel them, and slice them. Set the pressure cooker to" Sauté" mode.
2. Pour the olive oil into the pressure cooker and add the sliced carrots. Sprinkle the vegetables with the oregano and dill.
3. Sauté the dish for 15 minutes, stirring frequently. Sprinkle the carrot with the sugar, water, and sriracha. Mix well.
4. Close the pressure cooker lid and cook the dish on" Pressure" mode for 2 minutes. When the cooking time ends, release the remaining pressure and open the pressure cooker lid.
5. Transfer the carrots to a serving plate.

Nutritional Information: Calories 103, Carbs 10.2g, Fats 7g, Protein 1g

Vegan Mushroom Bourguignon

Preparation Time: 3hrs 10 mins

Servings: 4

Ingredients

- 250g white mushrooms
- 250g chestnut mushrooms
- 150g carrots
- 1 medium onion
- 3 cloves of garlic
- 1 tsp dried oregano
- 2 bay leaves
- 400ml vegetable stock
- 500ml vegan red wine
- 1 tbsp. tomato paste
- 2 tbsp. fresh thyme
- 2 tbsp. olive oil
- Salt and pepper to taste
- 3 tbsp. whole wheat flour

Instructions

1. Begin by preparing the vegetables, washing the mushrooms and carrots.
2. Slice the mushrooms into thick slices, dice the carrots into approx.2cm chunks, thinly slice the onion and crush the garlic.
3. Place all of the ingredients into the pot of your NINJA FOODI and mix to combine well.
4. Place the lid over the pot of the NINJA FOODI; select SLOW COOK on HI and cook for 2-3 hours.

5. Serve whilst warm and store the remaining in the fridge.

Vegan Chili

Preparation Time: 45 mins

Servings: 2

Ingredients

- 1/2 cup

- 2 medium potatoes

- olive oil

- garlic

- salt

- black pepper

- cayenne pepper

Instructions

4. 1/2 cup water in the pot, pierced two medium potatoes and cooked for 10 minutes at high pressure; used a quick release.

5. Brushed the potatoes with olive oil, garlic, salt, black pepper, and cayenne pepper; air crisped at 350°F for 10 minutes.

6. Bumped the temp up to 400°F and cooked for 15 minutes longer.

Potato Wedges

Serves: 4

Preparation Time: 40 minutes

Ingredients

- 1 lb. potatoes, sliced into wedges
- 1 tsp. olive oil
- Salt and pepper, to taste
- 1/2 tsp. garlic powder

Directions

5. Coat the potatoes with oil. Season with salt, pepper and garlic powder
6. Add the potatoes in the Ninja Foodi basket. Cover with the crisping lid. Set it to air crisp.
7. Cook at 400 degrees F for 16 minutes, flipping halfway through.
8. You can serve with vegan cheese sauce. Enjoy!

Nutritional Information: Calories 179, Carbs 36.2g, Fats 2.6g, Protein 2.8g

Ninja Foodi Steak Fries

Serves: 4

Preparation Time: 25 minutes

Ingredients

- 4 Russet Potatoes

- 1 tbsp slap yo mama (optional)

- 1 cup water

- 1/2 cup olive oil

Directions

1. Cut your potatoes into 1/2-inch wedges

2. Mix together Slap yo mama spices and olive oil

3. If you don't like the spicy seasonings you can use paprika, and garlic powder, salt pepper mixed with your olive oil.

4. Coat your fries with the seasonings

5. Place one cup water in the bottom of your foodi. Place fries in your air fryer basket

6. cook on high pressure for 10 minutes. Do a quick release

7. Remove the pressure cooker lid

8. Place on air crisp 400 degrees for 10 minutes. Open after 5 minutes to stir.

Roasted Vegetables with Tamarind Dip

Serves: 6

Preparation: 10 mins

Ingredients

- 1 cup potatoes, cubed
- 1 cup green bell pepper, cubed
- 1 cup carrots, sliced
- 1 cup onion, quartered
- 1 cup cauliflower florets
- 1/4 cup balsamic vinegar
- 1 tsp black pepper
- Salt to taste
- 1 cup broccoli florets
- 3/4 cup peas

For Dip

- 1/2 cup tamarind paste
- 1 clove garlic, minced
- 1/2 tsp black pepper

For Garnishing

- 1/4 cup sesame seeds

Directions

1. Mix all the dip ingredients to a bowl; set aside.
2. In a large mixing bowl, combine all the vegetables.
3. In another small mixing bowl, mix balsamic vinegar, black pepper and salt; mix until well combined.

4. Add the dressing into the vegetables, toss until they are well coated.

5. Preheat the foodi to air crisp mode, for 5 minutes.

6. Place the vegetables into the basket and bake/roast at 400F for 10 minutes.

7. When finished cooking, transfer the veggies to a serving dish. 8. Top with sesame seeds and serve with dip.

Nutritional Information: Calories 49, Carbs 10.52g, Fats 0.18g, Protein 1.59g

Chocolate Orange & Almond Granola

Prep: 20 mins/Cook: 30 mins

Servings: 4

Ingredients

- 200g oats
- 60g almonds
- 3 tbsp. coconut oil (melted)
- 4 tbsp. Orange Blossom Vegan Honea
- 1 heaped tbsp. cacao powder
- 1 tsp cinnamon powder
- Zest of 1/2 orange
- Pinch of salt

Instructions

1. Pre-heat the Foodi to 325F.

2. Add the almonds to your Ninja Kitchen food processor and pulse for a few seconds until the almonds are broken down into small pieces.
3. Add the almond pieces to a mixing bowl along with the oats, cacao powder cinnamon and pinch of salt.
4. Add the melted coconut oil, vegan honea and orange zest to the bowl and mix everything together well.
5. Spread the mixture onto Ninja multi-purpose baking pan evenly
6. When unit is preheated, place pan on reversible rack, making sure rack is the lower position. Place rack with pan in pot. Close crisping lid.

7. Select BAKE/ROAST, and set time to 20 minutes. Select START/STOP to begin.

8. Once baked allow the granola to cool completely before tucking in or transferring to an air-tight container to consume within 2 weeks.

Steamed Broccoli and Carrots with Lemon

Preparation Time: 10 minutes

Serves: 3

Ingredients

- 1 cup broccoli florets

- 1/2 cup carrots, julienned

- 2 tbsp. lemon juice

- Salt and pepper, to taste

Directions

5. Place the Ninja Foodi Cook and Crisp reversible rack inside the ceramic pot.

6. Pour water into the pot. Toss everything in a mixing bowl and combine. Place the vegetables on the reversible rack.

7. Close the pressure lid and set the vent to SEAL.

8. Press the Steam button and adjust the cooking time to 10 minutes. Do a quick pressure release. Serve and enjoy!

Nutritional Information: Calories 35, Carbs 8.1g, Fats 0.3g, Protein 1.7g

Asparagus and Chives

Preparation Time: 17 minutes

Serves: 4

Ingredients

- 1-pound asparagus, trimmed
- 2 tablespoons balsamic vinegar
- Salt and black pepper to the taste
- 1 tablespoon olive oil
- 2 tablespoons chives, chopped

Directions

1.   Put the reversible rack in the Foodi, add the baking pan and mix all the ingredients inside.

2.   Cook on Baking mode at 390 degrees F for 12 minutes, divide everything between plates and serve.

Nutritional Information: Calories 174, Carbs 12g, Fats 6g, Protein 7g

Crispy Cauliflower Bites

Preparation Time: 12 minutes

Serves: 4

Ingredients

- 3 garlic cloves, minced
- 1 tbsp. olive oil
- 1/2 tsp. salt
- 1/2 tsp. smoked paprika
- 4 cups cauliflower florets

Directions

8. Place in the ceramic pot the Foodi Cook and Crisp basket.
9. Place all ingredients in a bowl and toss to combine.
10. Place the seasoned cauliflower florets in the basket.
11. Close the crisping lid and press the Air Crisp button before pressing the START button.
12. Adjust the cooking time to 10 minutes.
13. Give the basket a shake while cooking for even cooking.
14. Serve and enjoy!

Nutritional Information: Calories 130, Carbs 7g, Fats 12.4g, Protein 4.3g

Cauliflower Stir Fry

Preparation Time: 40 minutes

Serves: 4

Ingredients

- 1 head cauliflower, sliced into florets
- 3/4 cup white onion, sliced
- 5 garlic cloves, minced
- 1 1/2 tsp. tamari
- 1 tbsp. rice vinegar
- 1/2 tsp. coconut sugar
- 1 tbsp. hot sauce

Directions

1. Put the cauliflower in the Ninja Foodi basket.
2. Seal the crisping lid.
3. Select the air crisp setting.
4. Cook at 350 degrees F for 10 minutes.
5. Add the onion, stir and cook for additional 10 minutes.
6. Add the garlic, and cook for 5 minutes. Mix the rest of the ingredients.
7. Pour over the cauliflower before serving.
8. You can garnish with chopped scallions. Enjoy!

Nutritional Information: Calories 93, Carbs 12g, Fats 3g, Protein 4g

Stewed Cabbage

Preparation Time: 40 minutes

Serves: 7

Ingredients

- 13 ounces cabbage
- 2 red bell pepper
- ¼ Chile pepper
- 1 cup tomato juice
- 1 tablespoon olive oil
- 1 teaspoon salt
- 1 teaspoon paprika
- 1 teaspoon basil
- ½ cup dill, chopped

Directions

4. Wash the cabbage and chop it into tiny pieces. Sprinkle the chopped cabbage with the salt, paprika, and basil and mix well using your hands.

5. Transfer the chopped cabbage in the pressure cooker. Add tomato juice, olive oil, and chopped dill. Chop the Chile pepper and red bell pepper.

6. Add the vegetables to the pressure cooker and mix well. Close the pressure cooker lid and cook the dish on" Pressure" mode for 30 minutes. When the dish is cooked, let it rest briefly and serve.

Nutritional Information: Calories 46, Carbs 6.6g, Fats 2.2g, Protein 1g

Teriyaki Glazed Aubergine

Prep: 40 mins

Servings: 8

Ingredients

- 1 large aubergine
- 1 tbsp. sesame oil
- 1 tbsp. tamari sauce
- 1 tbsp. agave syrup
- Pinch grated ginger
- 1 garlic clove - crushed
- Pinch chilli flakes
- 1/2 lime - juiced
- Sprinkle sesame seeds

Instructions

1. Slice the aubergine in half-length ways and score a Criss cross pattern over the inside of both pieces (this will help the marinade to absorb all the flavor)

2. Coat the aubergine in a tsp of sesame oil and rub this all over. Place the aubergine into the cooking basket with 150ml water in the bottom of the Ninja Foodi. Set to 'Air Crisp' at 375F and cook for 10 minutes.

3. Meanwhile, mix together the sesame oil, tamari, agave, ginger, garlic, lime and chilli flakes to make the marinade. Add a splash of water if needed. You want the mixture to be a little sticky.

4. Pour this over the aubergine and into all of the slits you made earlier, then cook for a further 15 minutes until beautifully soft and crisp around the edges.

5. Sprinkle with sesame seeds and serve!

Baked Bananas

Serves: 4

Preparation Time: 12 minutes

Ingredients

- 4 firm bananas, peeled and halved

- 1/4 cup maple syrup

- 1 tbsp. ground cinnamon

- 1-piece fresh ginger, grated

- 1 1/2 tsp. nutmeg

Directions

6. Place in the ceramic pot the Foodi Cook and Crisp reversible rack.

7. In a bowl, season the bananas with maple syrup, ground cinnamon, ginger, and nutmeg. Place the bananas on the rack.

8. Close the crisping lid and press the Bake/Roast button before pressing the START button.

9. Adjust the cooking time to 10 minutes.

10. Serve and enjoy!

Nutritional Information: Calories 183, Carbs 42.2g, Fats 0.9g, Protein 1.4g

Asparagus and Chives

Preparation Time: 17 minutes

Serves: 4

Ingredients

- 1-pound asparagus, trimmed

- 2 tablespoons balsamic vinegar

- Salt and black pepper to the taste

- 1 tablespoon olive oil

- 2 tablespoons chives, chopped

Directions

1.   Put the reversible rack in the Foodi, add the baking pan and mix all the ingredients inside.

2.   Cook on Baking mode at 390 degrees F for 12 minutes, divide everything between plates and serve.

Nutritional Information: Calories 174, Carbs 12g, Fats 6g, Protein 7g

Gluten Free Pasta with Pesto, Avocado and Coconut Yoghurt

Preparation Time: 25 mins

Servings: 4

Ingredients

Pesto

- 1 bunch Basil Leaves (about 20 grams)

- 30g walnuts

- 1 ripe avocado

- 2 tbsp. lemon juice

- 2 tbsp. Vegan coconut yogurt (or dairy alternative)

- 3 garlic cloves

- 100ml olive oil

- Salt & pepper, to taste

- Pasta

- 200g gluten free pasta (I used soy bean)

Toppings

- Toasted mixed nuts

- Baby plum tomatoes

- 2 tbsp. nutritional yeast (optional)

Directions

1. Cook pasta according to packet instructions, drain and set aside.

2. Add all the ingredients for the pesto to the blender and blend until a thick paste form.

3. Add the pesto to the pasta in a large pot and mix to combine.

4. If the pesto is too thick, add a little water to it.

5. Season and Top with Toasted mixed nuts, baby plum tomatoes and nutritional yeast.

Butternut Squash & Red Onion Dahl

Preparation Time: 15 mins

Servings: 1

Ingredients

- 300g butternut squash (peeled, chopped and de-seeded)
- 100g red onion (peeled and chopped)
- 400g red lentils
- 200g sweetcorn
- 200g spinach
- 500ml water
- 2 tsp vegetable stock powder (or 1 small stock cube)
- 2 tsp medium curry powder
- 1 tsp ground cumin
- 1 tsp ground coriander
- 1/2 tsp paprika

Direction

1. Add all of the ingredients, apart from the sweetcorn and spinach, to the Ninja Foodi and stir.
2. Place the Pressure Lid on your Ninja Foodi. Select 'pressure' for 5-8 minutes. Choose 5 minutes for firmer lentils and 8 minutes for a fluffier dahl.
3. Once the dahl is cooked be sure to release the pressure before opening the lid.

4. Stir in the sweetcorn and spinach, which will wilt and cook through with the heat of the dahl.

5. Leave it to cool slightly before serving.

6. Serve with brown rice, fresh coriander and a squeeze of lemon

Sticky Date & Ginger Flapjack

Preparation Time: 40 mins

Servings: 12

Ingredients

- 250g margarine

- 200ml maple syrup or date nectar

- 100g dates

- 50g coconut sugar

- 100ml orange juice

- 350g rolled oats

- 1 tsp ground ginger

- 1 tsp coconut oil

- 50g dark chocolate, broken up into pieces

Instructions

1. Set Foodi to Bake/Roast and Preheat the Foodi to 350 F

2. Grease and line an 8-inch baking pan.

3. Gently melt the margarine, maple syrup/date nectar and coconut sugar.

4. Place the dates in a pan with the orange juice and simmer for 5 minutes until softened. Allow to cool a little then place in your Ninja Kitchen Nutri Ninja blender along with the melted margarine mixture and blend to form a thick syrup mixture.

5. Place the oats and ginger in a bowl, add the date mixture and mix well until combined. Tip into the pan and press down evenly.

6. When unit is preheated, place pan on reversible rack, making sure rack is the lower position. Place rack with pan in pot. Close crisping lid. Select BAKE/ROAST, and set time to 20 minutes. Select START/STOP to begin.

7. Bake for 20 minutes until golden then leave to cool in the pan. After 10 minutes cut into 9-12 pieces but leave in the pan.

8. Gently melt the coconut oil and chocolate and drizzle over once cooled.

Buffalo Cauliflower Steak

Preparation Time: 45 mins

Servings: 2

Ingredients

- 1 head of cauliflower

- 1 cup of water

- 1 teaspoon olive oil

- 1 teaspoon lime chicken salt

- 2 cloves garlic, minced

- 2 teaspoons Franks RedHot seasoning powder

Instructions

4. Put 1 head of cauliflower and 1/4-ish cup of water in your Foodi and cook on low pressure for 3 minutes, quick release.

5. While the cauliflower was under pressure, prepare 1/2 cup sauce in a measure cup (1 teaspoon olive oil, 1 teaspoon lime chicken salt, 2 cloves garlic, minced, 2 teaspoons Franks RedHot seasoning powder, water).

6. After pressure is released, pour the buffalo sauce over the cauliflower. Air Crisp for 15 minutes at 390°F.

Crispy Artichokes

Preparation Time: 20 minutes

Serves: 4

Ingredients

- 3 cups artichoke hearts

- 2 tablespoons olive oil

- A pinch of salt and black pepper

- 1 tablespoon lemon juice

Directions

1.   In your Foodi's basket mix the artichoke hearts with the rest of the ingredients and cook them on Air Crisp at 400 degrees F for 15 minutes.

2.   Divide between plates and serve.

Nutritional Information: Calories 184, Carbs 10g, Fats 5g, Protein 6g

Vegan Chili

Preparation Time: 45 mins

Servings: 2

Ingredients

- 1/2 cup
- 2 medium potatoes
- olive oil
- garlic
- salt
- black pepper
- cayenne pepper

Instructions

7. 1/2 cup water in the pot, pierced two medium potatoes and cooked for 10 minutes at high pressure; used a quick release.

8. Brushed the potatoes with olive oil, garlic, salt, black pepper, and cayenne pepper; air crisped at 350°F for 10 minutes.

9. Bumped the temp up to 400°F and cooked for 15 minutes longer.

Buffalo Cauliflower Steak

Prep: 45 mins

Servings: 2

Ingredients

- 1 head of cauliflower

- 1 cup of water

- 1 teaspoon olive oil

- 1 teaspoon lime chicken salt

- 2 cloves garlic, minced

- 2 teaspoons Franks RedHot seasoning powder

Instructions

7. Put 1 head of cauliflower and 1/4-ish cup of water in your Foodi and cook on low pressure for 3 minutes, quick release.

8. While the cauliflower was under pressure, prepare 1/2 cup sauce in a measure cup (1 teaspoon olive oil, 1 teaspoon lime chicken salt, 2 cloves garlic, minced, 2 teaspoons Franks RedHot seasoning powder, water).

9. After pressure is released, pour the buffalo sauce over the cauliflower. Air Crisp for 15 minutes at 390°F.

Vegan Carrot Gazpacho

Preparation Time: 2 hr. 30 minutes

Serves: 4

Ingredients

- 1-pound trimmed carrots

- 1-pound tomatoes; chopped

- 1 red onion; chopped

- 2 cloves garlic

- 1 cucumber, peeled and chopped

- 1/4 cup extra-virgin olive oil

- 1 pinch salt

- 2 tablespoon lemon juice

- 2 tablespoon white wine vinegar

- salt and freshly ground black pepper to taste

Directions

1. Add carrots, salt and enough water to the Foodi. Seal the pressure lid, choose Pressure, set to High, and set the timer to 20 minutes. Press Start. Once ready, do a quick release.

2. Set the beets to a bowl and place in the refrigerator to cool.

3. In a blender, add carrots, cucumber, red onion, pepper, garlic, olive oil, tomatoes, lemon juice, vinegar, and salt. Blend until very smooth. Place gazpacho to a serving bowl, chill while covered for 2 hours.

Nutritional Information: Calories 88, Carbs 10.7g, Fats 4.7g, Protein 3.2`g

Green Lasagna Soup

Preparation Time: 30 minutes

Serves: 4

Ingredients

- ½ pound broccoli; chopped

- 3 lasagna noodles

- 1 carrot; chopped

- 2 garlic cloves minced

- 1 cup tomato paste

- 1 cup tomatoes; chopped

- ¼ cup dried green lentils

- 2 cups vegetable broth

- 1 cup leeks; chopped

- 1 teaspoon olive oil

- 2 teaspoon Italian seasoning

- salt to taste

Directions

4. Warm oil on Sear/Sauté. Add garlic and leeks and cook for 2 minutes until soft; add tomato paste, carrot, Italian seasoning, broccoli, tomatoes, lentils, and salt. Stir in vegetable broth and lasagna pieces.

5. Seal the pressure lid, choose Pressure, set to High, and set the timer to 3 minutes. Press Start.

6. Release pressure naturally for 10 minutes, then release the remaining pressure quickly. Divide soup into serving bowls and serve.

Nutritional Information: Calories 253.5, Carbs 22.8g, Fats 6.5g, Protein 24g

Vegetarian Shepherd's Pie

Preparation Time: 30 minutes

Serves: 7

Ingredients

- 2 white onions

- 1 carrot

- 10 ounces mashed potatoes

- 3 ounces celery stalk

- 1 tablespoon salt

- 1 teaspoon paprika

- 1 teaspoon curry

- 1 tablespoons tomato paste

- 3 tablespoons olive oil

- 1 teaspoon salt

Directions

1. Peel the carrot and grate it. Chop the celery stalk. Combine the vegetables together and mix well.

2. Put the vegetable mixture in the pressure cooker. Add the paprika, curry, tomato paste, olive oil, and salt. Mix well and stir well.

3. Cook at" Keep Warm" mode for 6 minutes, stirring frequently. Spread the vegetable mixture with the mashed potato and close the pressure cooker lid. Cook the dish on the" Pressure" mode for 10 minutes.

4. When the cooking time ends, release the pressure and open the pressure cooker lid.

5. Transfer the pie to a serving plate, cut into slices and serve.

Nutritional Information: Calories 104, Carbs 12g, Fats 6g, Protein 2g

Vegetarian Moroccan Red Lentil Soup or Stew

Preparation Time: 70 minutes

Serves: 1

Ingredients

- 2 Tbs. of olive oil

- 2 large onions

- 2 cloves of garlic

- 1 tsp fresh ginger

- 1 package of tempeh

- 2 tsp of ground coriander

- 1 tsp ground cumin

- 1 tsp ground turmeric

- ¼ tsp cinnamon

- salt to taste

- ½ tsp black pepper

- 7 cups of vegetable broth

- 1 can crushed tomatoes

- 1 jar of ethnic cottage Punjab spinach cooking sauce

- 2 cups dry red lentils

- juice of 1 lemon

- parsley and cilantro

Directions

1. Turn the Ninja to Stove Top High. Include the oil and sauté onions and garlic.

2. Include all flavors and tempeh. Blend well for 1 minute. Include soup and tomatoes.

3. Wash and deplete the lentils. Blend in the lentils, carrots, and kale.

4. Decrease the warmth to Stove Top Low for 60 minutes. Blend at times amid that time.

5. Rather than tomatoes this time; I utilized ethnic cabin Punjab spinach cooking sauce.

6. On the off chance that you include veggies it is increasingly similar to a stew and thicker.

7. You may need to include extra soup in the event that you include a lot of vegetables. Utilize your judgment.

Nutritional Information: Calories 574, Carbs 49.7g, Fats 19.3g, Protein 18.8g

Asian-Style Asparagus and Tofu Scramble

Preparation Time: 15 minutes

Serves: 2

Ingredients

- 1 tablespoon sesame oil

- 10 ounces soft silken tofu, drained and chopped

- 6 ounces asparagus

- 2 garlic cloves, finely minced

- 1 teaspoon fresh lemon juice

- 1 tablespoon soy sauce

- 1/2 teaspoon paprika

- 1/2 teaspoon coarse salt

- Freshly cracked mixed peppercorns, to taste

- 1/2 cup fresh basil, roughly chopped

Directions

1. Add 1 cup of water and a rack to the cooking pot. Place the asparagus on the rack.

2. Secure the pressure lid; press the STEAM button and cook for 2 minutes at High Pressure.

3. Once cooking is complete, use a quick release; remove the lid carefully.

4. Cut the cooked asparagus into pieces.

5. Stir in the other ingredients, except the basil leaves. Secure the crisping lid and choose the AIR CRISP function.

6. Set the temperature to 380 degrees F and set the time to 10 minutes; press the START/STOP button.

7. Serve warm garnished with fresh basil leaves. Bon appétit!

Nutritional Information: Calories 160, Carbs 8.5g, Fats 10.8g, Protein 8.9g

Clarion Wilson

Ratatouille

Preparation Time: 4 hours 40 mins

Serves: 1

Ingredients

- 2 Tbs. olive oil

- 3 cloves garlic

- 1 medium size onion

- 1 eggplant

- 2 zucchinis

- 2 red peppers

- 1 can diced tomatoes

- salt, pepper and a touch of oregano

- ¼ - cup of basil

Directions

1. Include garlic, peppers, eggplant, and zucchini to vessel.

2. Cook around 5-10 minutes until the point that somewhat delicate, yet at the same time somewhat fresh.

3. Include the tomatoes, and flavors.

4. Mix and Slow Cook Low for 4-4½ hours.

5. About ½ hour before done, when veggies are presently delicate, include the basil.

Nutritional Information: Calories 104.4, Carbs 15.1g, Fats 5g, Protein 2.4g

Cabbage Rolls

Serves: 1

Preparation Time: 1 hour

Ingredients

- 1 Whole cabbage

- 1½ cups wild rice

- 1 large carrot

- ½ onion

- 5 cloves garlic

- 2 cans tomato sauce

- 1 can tomato soup

- 4 cups vegetable stock

- salt and pepper

Directions

1. Add all fixings to the Ninja. Swing to Stove pinnacle High and warmth to the point of boiling.

2. Lessen warm temperature to Stove Top Low.

3. Cover and cook dinner for 40 - 50mins or till the point while rice is carried out and cabbage is delicate.

Nutritional Information: Calories 180.7, Carbs 22.2g, Fats 6.5g, Protein 8.1g